How to be Brilliant at
WRITING STORIES

Brilliant Publications

We hope you and your class will enjoy using this book. Other books in the series include:

English titles
How to be Brilliant at Writing Poetry	1 897675 01 1
How to be Brilliant at Grammar	1 897675 02 X
How to be Brilliant at Making Books	1 897675 03 8

Maths titles
How to be Brilliant at Algebra	1 897675 05 4
How to be Brilliant at Using a Calculator	1 897675 04 6
How to be Brilliant at Numbers*	1 897675 06 2
How to be Brilliant at Shape and Space*	1 897675 07 0

*To be published autumn 1994.

If you would like further information on these or other titles published by Brilliant Publications, write to the address given below.

Published by Brilliant Publications,
PO Box 143, Leamington Spa CV31 1EB

Written by Irene Yates
Illustrated by Kate Ford
Cover photograph by Martyn Chillmaid

Printed in Great Britain by the Warwick Printing Company Ltd

© Irene Yates 1993
ISBN 1 897675 00 3

Reprinted 1994

The right of Irene Yates to be identified as author of this work has been asserted by her in accordance with the Copyright, Designs and Patents Act 1988.

Pages 6–48 may be reproduced by individual teachers for class use, without permission from the publisher. All other material may not be reproduced in any form or for any purpose without the prior permission of the publisher.

Contents

Introduction	4
Links to the National Curriculum	5

The Process of Writing

Thinking	6
Getting ideas	7
Making notes	8
Plot table	9
Story outline	10
Character fact file	11
Redrafting	12
Ask a friend	13
Which way to publish?	14

Skills Development

Observation	15
Details, details	16
Keep a notebook	17
Words, words, words	18
Looking at change	19
Change that description!	20
Making plans	21
Every story has a BME!	22
In the beginning	23
Pile on the problems!	24
The end is near	25
Write together	26
Making up characters	27
Using a dictionary	28
Using a thesaurus	29
Punctuation	30
Making characters talk	31
Using speech marks	32
Learn to spell	33

Story Ideas

Stories I have read	34
Party madness!	35
Oh, to be on holiday!	36
Just imagine	37
Running free	38
What a brick!	39
Upside-down ideas	40
Keep going!	41
Motorway ideas	42
Time travel	43
Strange things	44
Letter stories	45
Keep a diary	46
Write a comic strip story	47
Glossary	48

Introduction

How to be Brilliant at Writing Stories contains 42 photocopiable ideas for use with 7–11 year olds. The book provides a flexible, but structured resource for developing writing skills, which both you and your pupils will enjoy.

The sheets are self-explanatory and ready to use; the only extra resources needed are a pen or pencil and sometimes extra paper. Word processing on the computer would be a bonus.

How to be Brilliant at Writing Stories supports many of the Programmes of Study for English in the National Curriculum (see page 5 for further details).

The book is divided into three sections:

The Process of Writing
The sheets in this section are open-ended and focus on the process of writing — from initial idea gathering to redrafting and final product. The sheets recognize that a sense of audience and a purpose for writing are crucial.

It is important that children feel ownership of their stories and understand that not all stories need to reach published form, and those which do can be produced in a variety of ways. Don't forget that sharing the stories aloud with the rest of the class is a form of publishing.

Skills Development
These sheets are designed to be used in conjunction with those in Section 1 as and when needed. Depending on the skills of your pupils, you may wish to use the skills sheets before the process ones, or vice versa.

It is important for the children to be able to practise the skills they have learned and one excellent way for them to do this is to have their own private notebook in which they can experiment.

Story Ideas
The ideas have been chosen to encourage children to write in a variety of different styles or genres. The sheets may provide starting points for the children's own ideas and need not be followed rigidly.

Links to the National Curriculum

The following Key Stage 2 Programmes of Study for English are covered in this book:

Pupils should:
- know for whom they are writing;

- have varied and frequent opportunities to write;

- show increased attention to the punctuation that demarcates sentences (capital letters, full stops, question marks and exclamation marks) and to the conventions of spelling;

- undertake chronological writing (for example, accounts of personal experiences, imaginative stories);

- be helped to increase their control of story form, through their experience of the stories they have read and heard, recognizing, for example, that the setting and the outcome need to be made explicit to the reader;

- be encouraged to be adventurous with vocabulary choices;

- be taught to use a thesaurus;

- be shown how to set out and punctuate direct speech;

- think about ways of making their meaning clear to their intended reader in redrafting their writing;

- be encouraged and shown how to check spellings in a dictionary or on a computer spelling checker when revising and proof-reading;

- be encouraged to find ways to reduce repetition in their own writing;

- be taught to recognize that writing involves:
    * decision-making — when the context (the specific situation, precise purpose and intended audience) is established;

    * planning — when initial thoughts and the framework are recorded and ordered;

    * drafting — when initial thoughts are developed, evaluated and reshaped by expansion, addition and amendment to the text;

- be taught to look for instances where:
    * meaning is unclear because of insufficient punctuation or omitted words;

    * meaning would be improved by a richer or more precise choice of vocabulary.

Thinking

Brilliant Writers love to sit around thinking. It might look as if they aren't doing anything, but really they are having a marvellous time thinking up good ideas for stories. Just imagine all the things you can make happen in your head that could never happen in real life!

Think now, and write down 20 ideas (no matter how silly they might seem). Some have already been done, just to get you going.

1. *If ants were as big as elephants*
2. *The fantastic frog jumping contest*
3. *Gerbils doing gymnastics*
4. *The toffee eating trophy*
5. *The day the clocks stopped*
6. _____
7. _____
8. _____
9. _____
10. _____
11. _____
12. _____
13. _____
14. _____
15. _____
16. _____
17. _____
18. _____
19. _____
20. _____

EXTRA!
Take your most interesting idea and develop it to make a story.

How to be Brilliant at Writing Stories

© Irene Yates
This page may be photocopied for use in the classroom only.

Getting ideas

I'm going to look for some ideas. Let me know if you see any...

Brilliant Writers know it's no good sitting down, waiting for ideas to come to them. Ideas don't work like that.
Brilliant Writers practise making ideas appear when they want them to.

Here's one way of doing it. Play the 'What if' game. Think of anything you like that's not ordinary.

What if ...

- ALL the supermarkets closed down?
- One day it rained custard?
- Senior citizens were sent to school?
- Children could...

EXTRA!
Choose one of your ideas to write up on the back of the sheet.
Save the rest for later.

© Irene Yates
This page may be photocopied for use in the classroom only.

How to be Brilliant at Writing Stories

Making notes

Making notes is *crucial* for a Brilliant Writer! If you don't make notes before you begin, how can you remember all the things you want to put in your story?

In the **Notes** box, jot down everything you can see in the picture. You don't have to write in sentences. Just write down words or phrases as they come to you.

Notes

Jot down here everything that might happen in your story:

EXTRA!
Now write up the story. Make it as dramatic and exciting as you possibly can!

How to be Brilliant at Writing Stories

© Irene Yates
This page may be photocopied for use in the classroom only.

Plot table

A good way to plan a story is to make a plot table.

Every story needs characters, a time it happens (past, present or future), a problem and a solution.

You can answer all these if you think of: Who? What? When? Where? and How?

Fill in the plot table for one of your story ideas.

Who?	
What?	
When?	
Where?	
How?	

EXTRA!
Make another plot table and fill it in for a well-known story.
You could write up both stories.

Story outline

Use this sheet to plan your story before you start to write.

Story title:

What happens in the beginning?

Who are you going to write your story for?

Who are your main characters?

What problems occur?

When and where does the story take place?

How will it end?

EXTRA!
You can use the back of the sheet to write your first draft.

How to be Brilliant at Writing Stories

© Irene Yates
This page may be photocopied for use in the classroom only.

Character fact file

You need to know your characters as well as you possibly can.

Decide who your character is and fill in the fact file.

You can make your character be whoever you like. Use the prompts around the edge of the sheet to help you.

Old? Young? Tall? Handsome? Pimply? Silent? Dreams of being rich? Dreams of saving the world? Dreams of being someone else?

What is your character's name?

What does your character look like?

What are your character's special qualities?

Cheerful? Neat? Scruffy? Naughty? Number of toes? Extra heads? Keeps a dragon? Clever? Bright?

EXTRA!
When you're sure you have a good character, work out a story-line and write up your story.

© Irene Yates
This page may be photocopied for use in the classroom only.

How to be Brilliant at Writing Stories

Redrafting

Choose a story you have written recently.

Read the whole thing aloud to a friend. Tell them to listen carefully to words, sentences, phrases and ideas.

What three things do they really like?

1

2

3

You can do this with all your stories.

What three things do they suggest you could change to improve the story?

1

2

3

Now edit your story!

EXTRA!
Here are some techniques you can use when editing your story.

- cross out words you don't want

  It was a ~~very~~ big dog.

- add in words wherever you want

  (best) my ^ friend came with me.

- change the order of words by drawing arrows

  Tom (ran) the other way (quickly).

- circle words you need to check in a dictionary or thesaurus

  then the (tyrannosaur) stomped across the valley.

- change the order of the sentences, or even the paragraphs!

  Use big arrows to do this!

How to be Brilliant at Writing Stories

Ask a friend

When you have finished your story, give it to a friend with this sheet. Ask them to comment on your story. When they have finished, talk about the story together.

This story is called...

It is written by...

I like this story because...

This story makes you want to read on because...

The best bit of the story is...

EXTRA!
Talk together about ways of improving the story — then make the changes!

© Irene Yates
This page may be photocopied for use in the classroom only.

How to be Brilliant at Writing Stories

Which way to publish?

Keep a list of stories you want to publish here:

How are you going to publish your story?

☐ using your best handwriting?

☐ using the computer?

Will you publish the story

☐ on its own?

☐ together with other stories in a collection?

Will you add

☐ a border?

☐ illustrations?

☐ a cover?

EXTRA!
Have you remembered to:
- share the story with a friend and ask for their comments?
- check that the story makes sense?
- check that the spelling and punctuation are correct?

How to be Brilliant at Writing Stories

© Irene Yates
This page may be photocopied for use in the classroom only.

Observation

A Brilliant Writer has to be good at observing things. It's no good writing 'The boy got dressed.' The reader wants to know more: What did he put on? What colour is his hair? Did he put anything on his feet?

You should know your key character so well that you could tell the reader all this and more — like what does he have for breakfast? does he have any horrible habits like nail biting? — even if they don't go in your story.

You get all these ideas by being observant. So, how observant are you? Answer this quiz— without cheating!

Observation quiz

1. What colour are your best friend's eyes?
2. How many lace holes are there in your shoes?
3. What hair-style does your teacher have?
4. What kind of floor is outside the school hall?
5. How many dinner ladies does your school have?
6. What can you see from your classroom window? (without looking!)
7. What colour is your next door neighbour's front door?
8. What was your best friend wearing yesterday?
9. How many litter bins are there in your playground?
10. How many post boxes do you pass on the way to school?

Check your answers and mark yourself out of 10 for observation!

EXTRA!
Set an observation quiz for a friend and give them a point for every correct answer.

© Irene Yates
This page may be photocopied for use in the classroom only.

How to be Brilliant at Writing Stories

Details, details

Brilliant Writers know that the smallest details are important.

Read this piece:

> Emma was out with the dog when a burglar got in and took all the valuable things. The police caught him.

That doesn't tell you much, does it? Ask yourself these questions:

- Who's Emma?
- Where was she going?
- Why didn't she leave the dog at home?
- How did the burglar get in?
- Why didn't the neighbours hear anything?
- What was stolen?
- How did Emma discover the break in?
- How did the police get involved?
- What happened next?

It's no good saying 'They went to town,' if you don't say who they are!

It's no good saying 'Emma and Brian had a dog,' if you don't say whether it is a lolloping, lip-smacking, tail-wagging, friendly kind of dog!

Now, write the story with all the details.

EXTRA!
On the back, or on another sheet, write the story of Emma and Brian's lolloping, lip-smacking, tail-wagging, friendly kind of dog!

How to be Brilliant at Writing Stories

© Irene Yates
This page may be photocopied for use in the classroom only.

Keep a notebook

Brilliant Writers always keep a notebook with them because ideas come at the silliest times!

If you don't write them down straight away, you'll forget them, so you always need to have your notebook with you.

Each space on this sheet is a page from a Brilliant Writer's notebook, with the beginning of an idea. Fill in the rest of each idea.

Better not forget this one!

Story about a caterpillar that wants to fly. It doesn't know that...	The baby next door gets out through the fence and...	Somebody's brother is hurt in an accident and...
An elephant moves into the empty house next door and...	When aliens take over the school...	Ten straw hats float all along the river and..

EXTRA!
When you've filled in all your ideas, discuss them with a friend.
Pick your favourite idea and make it into a story. Don't lose the others though.
Put them in your notebook to write up another day!

© Irene Yates
This page may be photocopied for use in the classroom only.

How to be Brilliant at Writing Stories

Words, words, words

Sometimes you can make your imagination work just by brainstorming words. For instance:

food
apples
bananas
supermarket
Shopping
fruit salad
party
basket
guests
disappointment!

Brainstorm an idea you have (you could choose one from around the edge of the page).

Surprises

Now write your story.

The rain forest

Continue your story on the back of the sheet.

Dinosaurs

Air pollution

EXTRA!
Leave a special place in your notebook for brainstorming words!

How to be Brilliant at Writing Stories

Looking at change

Every story you read is about something changing. Stories can have different kinds of changes:
- from bad to good
- a change of heart
- a change of situation
- a change of mind

A story without anything changing wouldn't be a story at all. It would just be a description.

Read this:

What's change got to do with stories?

EVERYTHING!

Morning in Bimbourne

The sleepy village street was silent at six o'clock in the morning. Tom, the newspaper boy, walked from house to house, shoving the newspapers into the letter boxes. The pavements shone after the rain. A stray dog crossed the road in search of something to eat. The sun peeped round the old church steeple. It looked like it would be a nice day.

Boring, eh? Make a list of ten possible things that could happen to change the sleepy village's day.

1
2
3
4
5

6
7
8
9
10

EXTRA!
Choose one of your ideas and write a story about what happens.

© Irene Yates
This page may be photocopied for use in the classroom only.

How to be Brilliant at Writing Stories

Change that description!

A description is a piece of writing that doesn't have any changes. Carry on writing this description. Remember, no changes!

Life at school was going on as usual. In the playground the pupils raced around. Some of them were playing football. Several children waited in a queue at the water fountain...

_____
_____
_____
_____
_____

Now write the same piece, but change something really dramatically. Make something happen!

Life was going on as usual. In the playground the...

_____
_____
_____
_____
_____
_____
_____

EXTRA!
With a friend, brainstorm a list of ideas for stories about school.
Choose one and write it together.

Making plans

Writing is a bit like going on a journey. You need to plan where you're going.

If you have a plan, you can see where your story will end up. Then you can write it from the beginning in the right direction.

Ask yourself six questions:

Who? What? Where? When? How? Why?

You can make up a table, like this:

Who	Jen, dog, burglar, next door neighbour, police
What	Mystery, Jen gone to vets, burglar breaks in, steals video and computer
Where	Sleepy village (Banham Green), motorway passes just by it
When	Present day, evening, early Autumn
How	Neighbour calls police, dog gets on trail, finds burglar at side of motorway waiting for lift
Why	Neighbourhood Watch campaign at work

You can see how the story would work, can't you? Now do a table for a story of your own. Think about it carefully.

EXTRA!
On the back of the sheet write up both stories.
You'll probably need more paper!

© Irene Yates
This page may be photocopied for use in the classroom only.

How to be Brilliant at Writing Stories

21

Every story has a BME!

Let's meet the BME — the three parts of any story:

I'm B - the beginning!

I set up the situation. I introduce the key character and show you what the problem is.

I'm M - the middle!

I show the key character struggling to solve the problem. This is where you can make things worse - heap more difficulties on the key character's head.

I'm E - the end!

I give the solution. The end will leave the key character changed and looking forward (hopefully!).

Think of a story you have read recently.

What happens?

At the beginning

In the middle

At the end

> **EXTRA!**
> When you write your own stories, make sure they have a BME — a beginning, a middle and an end!

How to be Brilliant at Writing Stories © Irene Yates

In the beginning

In the beginning of the story you need to introduce the key character, that's the main person in your story.

Decide who your key character is going to be and write down lots of details about her or him.

My key character is:

Details:

Don't forget the BME! 'B' – the beginning – comes first!

Then you need to decide what the key character's problem will be. This is what the story is all about.

My key character's problem is:

Write the beginning of your story here:

EXTRA!
You will get to write the middle and end later. Concentrate on the beginning for now.

Pile on the problems!

Remember the BME? Beginning, middle and end?

Right, now we're going to work on the middle of your story. The middle is where your character struggles to overcome whatever problem you've set up.

Go back to the beginning you wrote before. Make a note here of everything that could happen to make things worse.

You will need the beginning of the story you wrote earlier.

Choose one (or some) to use and write the middle of the story here. Remember to pile on the agony!

My key character is being bullied. How about yours?

Mine has followed an alien into space in a space capsule!

Wow! Maybe you could have the capsule take off.

Yeah! And your character could run away from school to escape the bully!

EXTRA!
You'll probably need more room, so use the back of the sheet!

How to be Brilliant at Writing Stories

© Irene Yates
This page may be photocopied for use in the classroom only.

The end is near

The end of the story has to solve all the problems in one fell swoop and it has to be satisfying to the reader. Get your beginning and middle together, read them through carefully.

Make a list here of every possible ending you can think of.

Remember! No cheating! The end has to fit the story!

Cross out any 'cheating' ones, like 'Then he woke up and found it was all a dream.' Write your ending here. Make sure there aren't any loose ends.

EXTRA!
Choose one of the other endings and write that too. Then read your story from beginning to both ends and choose which one fits best.

Write together

Write a story with a friend.

Write the beginning of your story here.

Adventure story idea – lost treasure

School story idea – getting into trouble

Now swap: your friend writes the middle here.

Space story idea – lost on Planet Z

Discuss the ending, then write it together here.

Animal story idea – no acorns for the squirrels

EXTRA!
Start a daily journal that you swap each day with a friend.
Write messages, stories and poems to each other and comment on them.

How to be Brilliant at Writing Stories

© Irene Yates
This page may be photocopied for use in the classroom only.

Making up characters

In any story you will usually find:
- a key character
- somebody on the side of the key character
- somebody against the key character

Take a story you know really well and write out three character fact files.

It might be a good idea to choose a story the whole class knows. Then you can compare fact files later.

Key character

Put all the ideas you can think of into your character fact files.

Person for

Person against

EXTRA!
When you've got the fact files worked out, turn the characters round and make a different person the key character. Think up another story-line and write it on the back of the sheet.

Using a dictionary

Brilliant Writers always make sure they're using the right words. Most writers have a shelf full of different dictionaries.

Get yourself a dictionary and use it to check both words and spellings.

Read this story:

I use my favourite dictionary all the time!

That's nothing! I've got 3 favourite ones!

Old Greedy Grimble

Old Greedy Grimble gazed out of the window at the precipitating elements. 'Oh dear!' he groaned, 'Doesn't look as if I'll get any laundry done!' But suddenly, to his surprise, there appeared before his eyes a multicoloured arc and it stretched — a magic spectrum— across his horticultural pleasure ground. Suddenly his fatigue vanished. 'Wow!' cried Old Greedy Grimble, 'There'll be a vast store of ore at the end of that, I'll be bound!' And he picked up his shovel.

Wow! Lots of difficult words in that — but it's a very simple story really. Look up the words you don't know in your dictionary, then write it here, in your *own* words.

EXTRA!
Have a go the other way round! Write a simple story
then try to find complicated words for some of the easy ones.
See if your friend can understand it! Use the back of the sheet.

How to be Brilliant at Writing Stories

Using a thesaurus

Synonyms are words that mean the same.

Antonyms are words that mean the opposite.

A thesaurus gives you lots of words but it's not quite the same as a dictionary because it doesn't tell you what the words mean. Instead, it gives you lots of alternative words that mean the same, or almost the same. They're called synonyms. A thesaurus also gives you opposites. They're called antonyms.

There's bound to be a thesaurus in your school. Like dictionaries you can get really easy ones and harder and harder ones. It will tell you in the front how to use it. Try to get familiar with it.

Look in a thesaurus to see if you can find several synonyms for each of the words on this list:

said

smile

sat down

got up

went out

good

nice

delicious

person

house

She said ... she whispered ... she muttered ... she shouted ... she ...

EXTRA!
Use a thesaurus, in your spare time, to learn ten new words every week.

© Irene Yates
This page may be photocopied for use in the classroom only.

How to be Brilliant at Writing Stories

Punctuation

Brilliant Writers always use punctuation.
Can you match these up correctly?

full stop
comma
exclamation mark
question mark
speech marks
colon
semicolon
hyphen

When you write a story, read it aloud to a friend to check you've got the punctuation right.

How many can you put into the next story? You will need to capitalize some of the letters as well.

crash

the biggest monster in the world was coming down the stairs three at a time dad was getting the breakfast he shouted stop that racket to my sister but she had already fainted on the floor the monster was pretty huge it had the look of a floating jelly all green and wobbly but i wasn't scared oh no not me what do you think you're doing here i asked it the monster grinned I've come for my breakfast it said i felt like people on toast today get out of this house i screeched go on get out but before i could say any more the monster had scooped me up and glug glug glug

EXTRA!
Make up your own Jelly Monster story on the back of the sheet and get your friend to put in the punctuation marks.

How to be Brilliant at Writing Stories

Making characters talk

Speech is sometimes called dialogue. If you get the punctuation wrong, your reader can't tell who's talking. Can you sort out who's saying what?

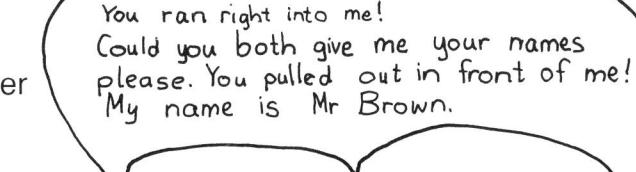

You ran right into me! Could you both give me your names please. You pulled out in front of me! My name is Mr Brown.

Now look at this muddle:

> Sam said it's a nice day today yes it is agreed Sue but it depends what you're going to do. I might go swimming. That's a good idea. Do you want to come as well? Well I'll have to ask my gran first but if I can I'll meet you down the road. She said that's okay. Are you coming then? Yes.

What a muddle! The rules for speech marks are easy:

speech marks go at the beginning, and the end, of everything somebody says.

Write the story with the speech marks in. The first bit is done for you:

Sam said 'It's a nice day today.'

> **EXTRA!**
> Make up two characters of your own, having a conversation. Draw it in speech bubbles first, then write it out, using speech marks.

© Irene Yates
This page may be photocopied for use in the classroom only.

How to be Brilliant at Writing Stories

Using speech marks

You already know that you need speech marks to show that someone's talking. There are a few more things to remember. The rules are these:

The words inside the speech marks always begin with a capital letter and end with a full stop or other punctuation mark.

Every time a different character speaks, you must start a new line or paragraph. Think of your speech marks as a kind of bubble in a comic strip — you wouldn't have two people speaking in the same bubble, would you? Neither do two people speak in the same speech marks.

Look at this comic strip:

Write these speeches into the bubbles.

'Hey Tom! That football's mine!'
'It's mine. Honest, I got it for my birthday.'
'Well — it looks like the one I lost last week.'
'It isn't — my mum bought it for me...'
'I don't believe you.'
'Come back! Oh no, now I'll be in trouble!'
'Guess it's not mine after all, mine bounced better than this!'
'Thanks. Do you want to join in the game?'

EXTRA!
Make up a cartoon with speech bubbles. Give it to a friend and ask him to write out the speech using speech marks. Check he's done it right!

How to be Brilliant at Writing Stories

© Irene Yates
This page may be photocopied for use in the classroom only.

Learn to spell

Brilliant Writers need to be good at spelling. Keep a section in your notebook for new words. Every time you find a word you haven't used before, jot it down. When you're reading you can often guess what a new word means from the sense of the sentence.

Learn how to spell a new word like this:

| Copy it out correctly on a piece of paper. | Break it down into syllables. Look at each syllable carefully. | Say each syllable aloud | Trace the letters with a pencil or with your little finger. |

All you need next is to test your memory.

Turn the piece of paper over and write the word. Then check it. If it's right, go on to the next word. If it's wrong, find out where you made the mistake and try again.

Practise with these words:

terrapin   beautiful   decision

Now, use a dictionary to make a list of ten new words, but don't make them too easy!

1
2
3
4
5
6
7
8
9
10

EXTRA!
When you've finished, work with a friend to test each other on your lists. Then you could set a new list for each other!

Use the rules to learn them, then test yourself.

© Irene Yates
This page may be photocopied for use in the classroom only.

How to be Brilliant at Writing Stories

Stories I have read

You can keep a record of the stories you read on this chart. Every time you read a story, add it to the chart.

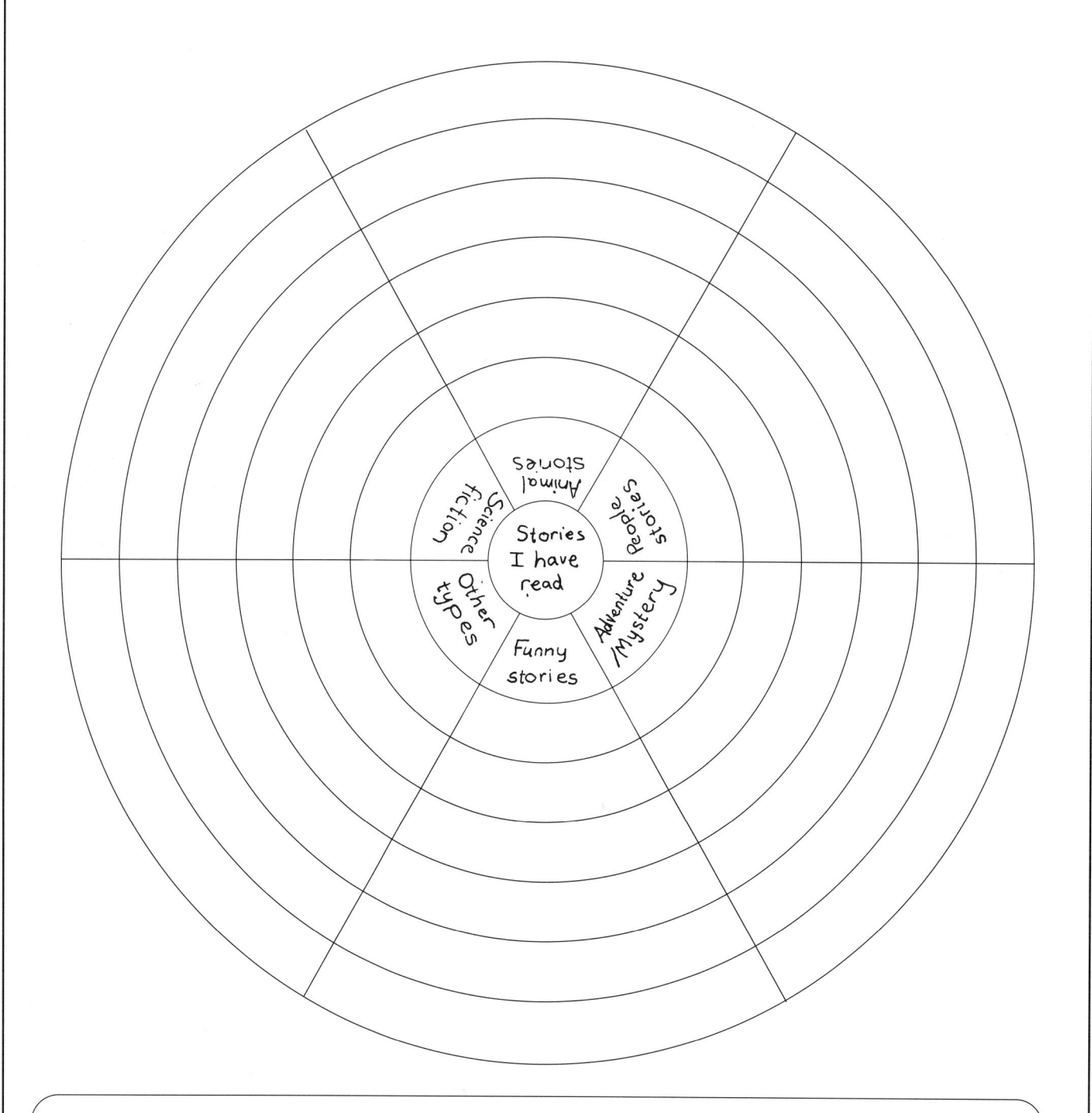

(Chart categories: Stories I have read — Animal stories, People stories, Adventure/Mystery, Funny stories, Other types, Science fiction)

EXTRA!
Pick two stories from your chart. What would happen if the characters met?
Write a story about what happens.

How to be Brilliant at Writing Stories © Irene Yates
This page may be photocopied for use in the classroom only.

Party madness!

Brilliant Writers try to use all their senses when writing. That way they can make their stories really interesting to the reader.

Put yourself into party-going mode. Make notes here for:

Whose party?

Where is it?

When is it?

How are you getting there?

What kind of party?

Why are you going?

Gosh, that cake looks nice!

Turn that music down!

Yuck! I can't stand the taste of this stuff!

Poooh! What's that smell?

This wrapping paper feels really silky!

(You don't have to be just an ordinary person. You can be anything or anyone you like!)

Now write your party story, making sure that you use all of the five senses to help the reader capture the feel of being there.

EXTRA!
Think back to a party you went to, and describe all the sights, sounds, tastes, smells and textures you can remember.

Oh, to be on holiday!

Everybody loves holidays. You might holiday:

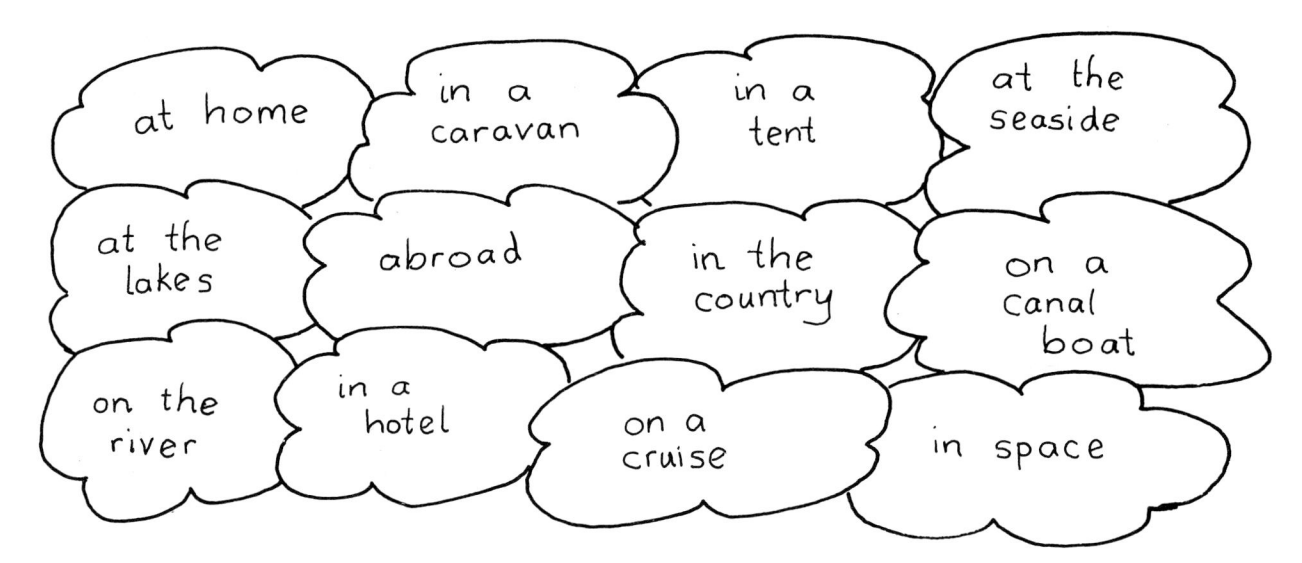

- at home
- in a caravan
- in a tent
- at the seaside
- at the lakes
- abroad
- in the country
- on a canal boat
- on the river
- in a hotel
- on a cruise
- in space

Choose a kind of holiday you'd really like to have. Make up a character.

This character is going to go on your holiday for you, and is going to have the biggest adventure of all time. Now what do you think might happen?

EXTRA!
Share your story with a friend. Write another one together.

How to be Brilliant at Writing Stories

© Irene Yates

This page may be photocopied for use in the classroom only.

Just imagine

Just imagine what would happen if your tame domestic pet suddenly grew as big as a wild animal.

Just imagine...
...little Pussikins, suddenly a huge, roaring tiger!

...little Goldie, swimming round in her fish tank, turning into a huge, sharp-toothed piranha!

...George the gerbil, bursting out of his cage as a monster mammoth!

Choose one, write one!

EXTRA!
Imagine your great big fierce guard dog shrinks to the size of an insect.
Write what happens.

Running free

"I'm a rabbit. I live in a hutch in a classroom. Pretty boring really."

"But today someone has left the door open. I've just noticed. It's playtime so there's no one around..."

What happens next? Write your story here.

"You could give your rabbit a name."

"Maybe you are the rabbit!"

"What if the headteacher comes into the classroom?"

EXTRA!
Instead of being the rabbit, be one of the children. You'll probably have to turn over the page. Or, be another kind of animal, and make up another story.

How to be Brilliant at Writing Stories

© Irene Yates
This page may be photocopied for use in the classroom only.

What a brick!

> Hello! I'm a brick. For the past 50 years I've sat happily in the wall of a house. But yesterday along comes a truck up the road, skids across and knocks my wall down.
>
> The house had to be demolished! I got thrown on a skip...

What happens next? You can see this is going to be a funny story, can't you?

Write your story here:

EXTRA!
Write a story about some other non-living thing: a boat, a car, a computer, a telephone, a ...

Upside-down ideas

When you want to write a funny story, it helps to have an unusual idea. You can get lots of them from thinking about other stories you have read and changing things. Try turning an idea upside down.

Cinderella is the story of a poor little girl who nobody loved. She became rich. Maybe you could write about somebody very rich who loved everybody — so she gave everything she had away and become poor.

The Owl who was Afraid of the Dark is a story about an owl who was frightened of growing up. Maybe you could write a story about someone old (a grandfather, perhaps) who discovered a magic formula for becoming young again. All was fine, till he had to go to school!

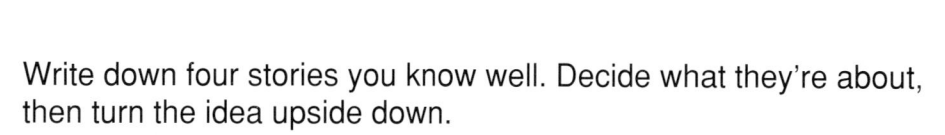

Write down four stories you know well. Decide what they're about, then turn the idea upside down.

Story	Upside-down idea

EXTRA!
Write up the one you like best. Save the rest for later.

Keep going!

Think of all the ways you can move. Maybe you can walk, run, hop, skip, jump.

Maybe you can skateboard!

Maybe your wheels go round very fast.

Maybe your wheels don't have brakes.

Maybe...Mum sends you to the shops and doesn't notice....

Maybe...

Write the story here:

CRASH!
Watch those tins!

CRASH!
Get out of the way!

CRASH!
Mind the cabbages!

CRASH!
What do you think you're playing at?

EXTRA!
The government announces that tomorrow is National Hopping Day!
Everyone has to hop everywhere — no walking or running allowed!
Write what happens.

Motorway ideas

You can get loads of ideas from watching the traffic on the motorway as you go along. Have you noticed how people keep overtaking you, then fall behind and catch you up again?

You could write a mystery
Who is in the red car that keeps trying to catch up with you? Why is the boy in the back signalling frantically? What's going to happen?

You could write an adventure
When you stop at the motorway services you recognize the man in the check shirt as the one who raced out of the petrol station with the owner chasing after him.

Choose and write *now*.

EXTRA!
Suppose the rules were changed and we suddenly had to drive on the right hand side of the motorway. Write the story.

Time travel

It's all very well having a home to go to. But what about if you got there, and your home had disappeared? And in its place was a field? Oak trees. Bushes. The neighbours had gone as well. In fact, all that was left was an Anglo-Saxon village half a mile away and a boy in a strange tunic who thought you'd come from another world.

It's no use yelling 'Mum!' What are you going to do now?

Write your story here:

EXTRA!
Suppose you were the boy in the strange tunic who lived in the Anglo-Saxon village. What's he going to think about *you*? Write his story!

Strange things

A good starting point for stories is to take something very, very ordinary and mix it with something strange. For instance:

You're taking the dog for a walk through the woods and you meet Mrs Jones who has her pet dragon on a lead. The lead breaks...

Or...

The school bus collects the class to take them swimming but instead of stopping at the baths the bus driver goes rushing off to the nearest port, races on to a ferry, and off you go across the sea to...

Or...

The ice-cream lady turns up in her van without any ice-cream, but she's doing a very nice line in Luscious Monster Dragon Toenail Clippings...

Write one of the stories here:

EXTRA!
Share your story with your friend. Write another one on the back!

Letter stories

Brilliant Writers can write super letter stories, just by having two people write to each other, the letters going backwards and forwards, backwards and forwards, so that the story's being told as they go. For example:

> Dear Susie,
> I heard you had an accident in the supermarket on your skateboard. I thought...

> Dear Rakesh,
> You're right about the accident. They told me not to go in on my skateboard, but I couldn't stop and Mum wanted...

> Dear Susie,
> Is your chin getting any better? What...

Think up two characters. Write their letters to each other. Make sure you've got a good story-line to unfold. Try to make it funny.

EXTRA!
If you've got lots of writing time left, finish off Susie and Rakesh's story.

© Irene Yates
This page may be photocopied for use in the classroom only.

How to be Brilliant at Writing Stories

Keep a diary

Dear Diary, Please make me as famous as Adrian Mole...

Keeping a diary can be a good starting point for a story. Especially if the diary doesn't belong to you. Suppose you were somebody else — a witch for instance, or a wizard, or an alien sailing through space?

Choose one of these characters to be (or make up one of your own) and keep a week's diary notes here.

Use your notes to help you write a story.

Who are you?
What were your plans?
Why did they go wrong?
Any surprises?
Any mysteries?
How did the weather affect your plans?

Monday

Tuesday

Wednesday

Thursday

Friday

Saturday

Sunday

Monday again...

What was good about the day?
What was bad about the day?
What were you looking forward to?
What were you dreading?

When you've finished your diary notes, write up your story on the other side of the sheet.

EXTRA!
Keep the same diary details but turn yourself into a different character,
or swap diaries with a friend but be your own character!
Then write another story!

How to be Brilliant at Writing Stories

© Irene Yates
This page may be photocopied for use in the classroom only.

Write a comic strip story

[Comic strip with four frames:]
Frame 1: "What are you doing?"
Frame 2: "I'm writing a comic strip."
Frame 3: "But don't you have to draw the pictures?" "No, the illustrator does that."
Frame 4: "Oh!"

This is how you write a comic strip. Each box is called a frame.

Each frame may contain:
- an illustration
- speech or thought bubble
- a caption

For each frame you willl need to work out what the picture will be and what the speech bubble and caption will say.

Write you own comic strip here:

Frame 1

Picture:

Speech bubble:

Caption:

Frame 2

Picture:

Speech bubble:

Caption:

Frame 3

Picture:

Speech bubble:

Caption:

Frame 4

Picture:

Speech bubble:

Caption:

You can add more frames if you like!

EXTRA!
Make a series of boxes and draw your cartoon!

© Irene Yates
This page may be photocopied for use in the classroom only.

How to be Brilliant at Writing Stories

Glossary

alphabetical order
Organized in the same order as the alphabet, with A coming first and Z last (like this glossary).

antonym
A word that means the opposite (or nearly the opposite). For example: good — bad, naughty.

audience
In writing stories your audience is the person or people who will read or listen to your story.

caption
The explanation of what's happening, in the frame of a picture story or cartoon strip.

character(s)
The person (or people) in your story.

description
Tells the reader what something or someone is like; gives background information.

dialogue
A conversation between two or more characters.

dictionary
A book, organized alphabetically, containing words and their meanings.

draft
When you 'draft' you write a piece, knowing you can change it. You may redraft a piece several times before you're happy that you have a final product.

edit
When you 'edit' you go through your piece of writing, looking for where you can correct or improve it.

frame
The boxes in a picture story or cartoon strip.

genres
Different types of writing, for example: science fiction, mystery, poetry, nonfiction.

picture story
This is sometimes called a cartoon strip. The story is shown by a series of pictures in frames.

presentation
How you make your piece of writing look. For example: neat, coloured in, with or without borders.

publish
To produce stories (or other types of written work) to be read by other people.

speech bubble
Usually in picture stories or cartoon strips; they show what a character is saying.

speech marks
Punctuation marks used to show when a character is speaking. The are used at the start and the end of whatever the character is saying.

story-line
A sentence that sums up what the story is all about.

synonym
A word that means the same thing (or nearly the same thing). For example: good — lovely, nice.

thesaurus
A book that gives synonyms and antonyms for words.

How to be Brilliant at Writing Stories